Wild Nature

SMELLY
and
Slow

Heinemann
LIBRARY

Elizabeth Laskey

www.heinemann.co.uk/library
Visit our website to find out more information about **Heinemann Library** books.

To order:
 Phone 44 (0) 1865 888066
 Send a fax to 44 (0) 1865 314091
 Visit the Heinemann Bookshop at www.heinemann.co.uk/library to browse our catalogue and order online.

First published in Great Britain by Heinemann Library, Halley Court, Jordan Hill, Oxford OX2 8EJ, part of Harcourt Education. Heinemann is a registered trademark of Harcourt Education Ltd.

© Harcourt Education Ltd 2005
First published in paperback in 2006
The moral right of the proprietor has been asserted.

Editorial: Barbara Katz and Kathy Peltan
Design: Kimberly Saar and David Poole
Picture Research: Bill Broyles
Production: Camilla Smith

Originated by Ambassador Litho Ltd
Printed in China by WKT Company Ltd.

ISBN 0 431 00234 7 (hardback)
09 08 07 06 05
10 9 8 7 6 5 4 3 2 1

ISBN 0 431 00239 8 (paperback)
10 09 08 07 06
10 9 8 7 6 5 4 3 2 1

British Library Cataloguing in Publication Data
Laskey, Elizabeth
Wild Nature: Speedy and Slow
578.4
A full catalogue record for this book is available from the British Library.

Acknowledgements
The publishers would like to thank the following for permission to reproduce photographs:
p. **4** Tom Brakefield/DRK Photo; p. **5** M. Harvey/DRK Photo; p. **6** Norbert Wu/DRK Photo; p. **7** Michael Fogden/DRK Photo; p. **8** Dietmar Nill/Nature Picture Library; p. **9t** Stephen J. Krasemann/DRK Photo; p. **9b** Partridge Films Ltd./Oxford Scientific Films; p. **10** Charles Bennett/AP Wide World Photo; p. **11** Lynda Richardson/Corbis; p. **12** Joe McDonald/DRK Photo; p. **13** Anthony Bannister/NHPA; pp. **14, 15** Martin Harvey/DRK Photo; p. **16** Tui De Roy/Minden Pictures; pp. **17, 24** Stephen Dalton/NHPA; p. **18** Paul Franklin/Oxford Scientific Films; p. **19** Joe McDonald/Corbis; p. **20** Avi Klapfer/Seapics.com; p. **21** George D. Lepp/Corbis; p. **22** Rob Nunnington/OSF/DRK Photo; p. **23** Ashok Jain/Nature Picture Library; p. **25** B. G. Thomson/Photo Researchers, Inc.; p. **26** Pete Oxford/DRK Photo; p. **27** D. Cavagnaro/DRK Photo; p. **28** David A. Northcott/Corbis; p. **29** David Sieren/Visuals Unlimited

Cover photograph of a cheetah by Corbis; inset photograph of snail by Dinodia Picture Agency/Oxford Scientific Films

Every effort has been made to contact copyright holders of any material reproduced in this book. Any omissions will be rectified in subsequent printings if notice is given to the publishers.

Contents

Some words are shown in bold, **like this.** You can find out what they mean by looking in the glossary.

Which big cat lives life in the fast lane?

Some plants and animals take their time. Others zip along at incredible speeds. In this book, you will meet a cat as fast as a car and a flower that takes up to 100 years to bloom. You will also find out how a plant or animal's speed (or the lack of it) can affect the way it lives and how it survives.

Meet the cheetah

The cheetah is the world's fastest land **mammal.** This big cat's body is sleek and its legs are long. These **adaptations** help the cheetah get up to a top speed of 113 kilometres (70 miles) per hour. The cheetah's flexible spine helps it stretch its body so it can cover long distances with each leap. A cheetah can cover about 7 metres in a single bound. That's about the length of a small caravan!

The cheetah can go from 0 to 72 kilometres (45 miles) per hour in a few seconds. But it can run at its top speed only for a short time – less than a minute.

In the wild many cheetah babies die before they are fully grown. This is another reason why the number of cheetahs has fallen.

The need for speed

Cheetahs are **predators** that live on the plains of Africa and in the Middle East. Gazelles often fall **prey** to cheetahs. These animals are nearly as fast as the cheetah, so the cheetah has to work hard for a meal. Being fast also helps the cheetah avoid danger. The cheetah does not have powerful jaws and teeth. When it faces danger, the cheetah runs instead of staying and fighting.

The cheetah's worst enemy

Farmers have killed cheetahs because they sometimes kill farm animals. Also, people have taken over much of the land where cheetahs hunt. In the mid-1970s, there were probably about 15,000 cheetahs in the world. Some scientists think there might have been as many as 25,000. Today, there are only about 12,000 left.

The cheetah is an **endangered species.** People are working to save the cheetah. They are protecting cheetah **habitat** and trying to **breed** cheetahs in captivity.

Who is the laziest mammal?

The three-toed sloth sleeps for nineteen hours a day. During the five hours a day that it tries to keep its eyes open, it still does not do much. If you think the sloth sounds lazy, you are not the first person to think this. The word *slothful* actually means 'lazy'.

A sloth uses its strong claws to hang on to tree trunks and branches and to pull itself slowly along.

Just hanging around

The three-toed sloth is a **mammal** that lives in the **rainforests** of Central and South America. It does almost everything it needs to do from its perch high in the trees. When a sloth is hungry, it eats a few leaves or twigs off the tree it lives in. When it needs a **mate,** it looks no further than a nearby tree. When it is sleepy (which is most of the time), it falls asleep hanging upside down from a branch! Sloths have special hooklike claws that let them hang safely from the branches.

On dangerous ground

Once a week the three-toed sloth climbs down to the ground to **urinate** and **defecate.** This is the most dangerous thing a sloth does. Its curved claws are an excellent **adaptation** for grasping tree branches. But they are no help on the ground. Their shape keeps the sloth from being able to walk or stand.

It takes the sloth about half an hour to dig a hole, urinate and defecate and then cover up the waste. During this time it is in danger of attack by **predators** such as jaguars.

Back in the trees, there is less danger. The sloth moves so little that green algae grows on its fur. This greenish fur helps **camouflage** the sloth. Predators have a hard time telling sloths apart from the leafy, green tree branches.

Baby three-toed sloths cling to their mothers for about six months.

Which daredevil bird is as fast as a racing car?

No bird is faster than the peregrine falcon. When flying, it can reach 97 kilometres (60 miles) per hour. That is the speed limit of a car on an open country road. But when dive-bombing **prey**, it reaches speeds of almost 322 kilometres (200 miles) per hour, or as fast as a racing car!

Peregrine falcons live in all parts of the world except Antarctica. They often build their nests on cliffs that are near water, so they can catch ducks and seabirds.

The peregrine falcon is an expert hunter. It makes a steep, fast dive, called a stoop. Then it hits its prey in midair with its sharp talons. The prey is often killed instantly. If not, the falcon kills the prey with a bite to the back of its neck.

During regular flight, the peregrine falcon moves at about 65 kilometres (40 miles) per hour.

Peregrine falcons become endangered

In the mid-20th century, the number of peregrine falcons around the world began to drop. By the 1960s, only about 360 pairs were left in the UK. Scientists discovered that the birds' bodies contained high amounts of the chemical DDT.

DDT is a poison sprayed on crops to keep insects away. Small birds ate insects that had DDT in their bodies. The falcons ate the birds and got the DDT in their bodies. DDT made the falcon's eggshells very thin. The eggs often broke before they could hatch. When adult falcons died, there were not enough baby falcons to take their place. The population of peregrines fell so far that they were listed as an **endangered** species.

A female peregrine falcon can lay as many as three or four eggs in spring. It takes about a month for the eggs to hatch.

The fastest bird on land

The ostrich of Africa cannot fly, but it can run very fast. It has long legs that let it take giant 4.5-metre steps. Ostriches can reach a speed of about 64 kilometres (40 miles) per hour. That's almost as fast as a galloping racehorse.

The falcons bounce back

The governments of western countries began working on plans to keep peregrine falcons from becoming **extinct.** They passed laws that made it illegal to use DDT on crops, and they took action to protect peregrine habitats.

A mother peregrine falcon stands over one of her chicks at a nest on an apartment building in Chicago, USA.

In the USA, scientists began **breeding** peregrine falcons in captivity. Between 1974 and 1999 about 6000 falcons were raised. Later they were placed in the wild. Often the 'wild' places were cities. The falcons were able to nest on bridges or the ledges of skyscrapers. This programme was extremely successful, and the population increased.

In the UK the peregrine population has also increased. In 2000, London's first breeding pair produced young on Battersea Power Station, overlooking the River Thames.

The peregrine falcon is not **endangered** any more. Its survival is an important conservation success story.

Which bird is a slow motion show-off?

It has been called a timberdoodle, bog sucker and mud bat. It is the American woodcock, the slowest flying bird in the world. It lives in forests from the eastern to the central parts of North America.

The American woodcock's eyes are set way back on its head This lets it see in every direction, even behind itself.

During the day the American woodcock hides. Its brown colour and dark markings help it blend in with the twigs and dry leaves. It uses its long beak to pull earthworms out of the soil.

Slow dancing

In spring the male American woodcock does a 'sky dance' to win a **mate.** Flying at about 8 kilometres (5 miles) per hour, he spirals up to about 75 metres. You would need binoculars to see him.

When he spirals upwards, you can hear a twittering sound. This is made by the three outer feathers on each wing. He circles for a bit. Then he zigzags back down, landing near where he took off. He repeats the show again and again, for up to 45 minutes.

Which is the fastest snake?

The black mamba is a **reptile** that lives in South Africa and central Africa south of the Sahara desert. It is usually about 2.7 metres long but can grow as long as 4.3 metres. That is about as long as a small car. It can zoom along at a speed of 11 kilometres (7 miles) per hour. That is almost as fast as some people can run.

The black mamba can unhinge (take apart) its jaws to open its mouth wide. This allows it to swallow prey that is up to four times the size of the snake's head.

The black mamba strikes

The black mamba sometimes wraps itself around tree branches, where it can hunt and catch birds. It also slithers quickly along the ground in search of other types of **prey** such as small **mammals.** To make a kill, it lunges quickly and sinks its fangs, or pointed teeth, into the victim. Poisonous venom flows into the prey. It is killed almost instantly.

The black mamba and humans

The black mamba has no animal **predators.** Its only real enemy is a human with a weapon. Black mambas do not go out of their way to attack humans. Usually a black mamba will speed away from a human and hide. But it will bite a human if it feels it is in danger and cannot escape.

If the black mamba attacks, it lifts as much as 1.2 metres of its body off the ground. It opens its mouth and flares out its head. It then quickly bites the human in the neck or chest.

The person must be given a medicine, called antivenom, that will keep the venom from working. Without this medicine, the bite can kill the person within twenty minutes.

The black mamba's skin is not black. Its name describes the colour of the inside of its mouth.

Which tortoises are never in a hurry?

The Galápagos islands, west of Ecuador in South America, are home to the Galápagos tortoises. These huge tortoises stroll along no faster than 0.26 kilometres (0.16 miles) per hour. It would take one about 30 minutes to walk the length of a football pitch. It would take you only a couple of minutes.

Giant Galápagos tortoises

There are eleven living **subspecies** of Galápagos tortoises. Most of these are very large. The largest can weigh more than 227 kilograms. They have a shell measuring 1.5 metres across. These tortoises can live for 150 years.

*In a study of captive Galápagos tortoises, it took twelve days for them to **digest** their food.*

Like all **reptiles**, the tortoises are **cold-blooded.** To get warm, they **bask** in the Sun. If they get too hot, they find some shade or a water hole so they can cool down. When they are hungry, they wander off to eat grasses, cacti or fruit.

Perfectly adapted

Each subspecies has **adaptations** that help it live in the **habitat** of a different Galápagos island. Tortoises with dome-shaped shells live where there is plenty of food that is easy to reach. But saddle-backed tortoises live on dry islands were food can be scarce. Their shells are shaped so that they can lift their heads high. This lets the tortoises eat both tall plants and those close to the ground.

Trouble for tortoises

European sailors and explorers came to the Galápagos islands in the 1500s. Before that time, the tortoises had few **predators.** But the sailors caught the tortoises and put them on their ships. During their travels, they killed the tortoises and ate them. By the mid-1900s, 100,000 to 200,000 Galápagos tortoises had been killed.

In 1959 the government of Ecuador made the islands a national park. This meant that the tortoises and their habitat could not be harmed. But some **subspecies** had already become **extinct.**

Galápagos tortoises are only about 5 centimetres long when they hatch. They can take as long as a month to dig their way out of the nest.

*This is 'Lonesome George', the only member of the Pinta Island **subspecies** of Galápagos tortoises. When he dies the Pinta Island subspecies will be **extinct**.*

Scientists have taken steps to help increase the tortoise population. They gather eggs and put them in a protected place to hatch. This way they will not get eaten by the dogs, rats and wild pigs that now live on the islands. When the baby tortoises are big enough, they are put back in the wild. Today there are about 15,000 giant tortoises living on the islands of the Galápagos. But most of the subspecies are still listed as **endangered.**

Did you know?

The word *galápago* means 'tortoise' in Spanish.

Can frogs fly?

In southeast Asian rainforests, some frogs seem to fly. They do not really fly, but they do move quickly through the air. The Wallace's flying frog can glide up to 15 metres.

Why fly?

A flying frog has webs of skin between all its toes. This **adaptation** helps the frog 'fly'. All it has to do is spread its toes and leap from a tree branch. This is a great way for the frog to make a quick getaway when a **predator** gets too close.

When flying frogs 'fly', they land lower than where they started. This is a Wallace's flying frog.

Did you know?

Another fake flyer

The Japanese giant flying squirrel can fly as far as 46 metres, or half the width of a football field.

Which amphibians are slow and slower?

Newts look a lot like lizards. But newts crawl along so slowly on land that it is easy to catch them. Lizards are fast. They can usually escape if someone tries to catch them.

In and out of the water

The big difference between a lizard and a newt is that a lizard is a **reptile** and a newt is an **amphibian** called a salamander. Newts live in moist areas in Europe, Asia and North America.

Newts start their life in water when a female newt lays eggs in a pond or stream. The **larvae** that hatch look a bit like fish. They live in water and breathe through **gills.** Slowly they grow legs. They also grow lungs so they can breathe on land. This change is called a **metamorphosis**.

The great crested newt which lives in Britain is only 10 to 15 centimetres long. Some newt larvae need as long as three months to undergo metamorphosis.

While living on land, newts are called efts. Efts are too slow to chase **prey.** They wait for a slow-moving animal, such as a slug or earthworm, to creep by. Then they grab it.

Great escapes

Newts can be prey for other animals. Turtles, snakes and birds may try to eat them. Newts are usually too slow to get away. But they have other ways to protect themselves. Their skins can ooze poison. The rough-skinned newt has enough poison to kill several adult humans. It lives in the western United States and Canada. If a **predator** grabs a newt, the newt can let its tail or even a leg snap off in the predator's mouth. The body part will grow back later.

The red spots on the red-spotted newt warn predators that the newt is poisonous.

Did you know?

In some newts, the eft stage can last one to seven years.

Which fish is a good sailor?

Sailfish are the fastest fish in the world. They can swim at 109 kilometres (68 miles) per hour. This is faster than the speediest sailing boats! They live in the Atlantic, Pacific and Indian Oceans.

Measuring about 3.4 metres long, a fully grown sailfish is about as long as a small sailing boat.

Growing fast too

Sailfish grow up fast, too. Their eggs hatch in only about a day and a half. Salmon eggs can take up to four months to hatch. A baby sailfish grows quickly, feeding on squid, octopus and fish. At the age of one year, it may already be 1.8 metres long, or the size of a fully-grown man.

The sailfish's 'sail' is a **dorsal fin** that is twice as tall as the fish's body. Scientists think the fin may be one of the reasons why the sailfish is faster than any other fish in the sea.

Who has thousands of feet and is still slow?

Starfish are **echinoderms.** Each of the starfish's arms has thousands of tiny tube-shaped feet. These tube feet help the starfish creep slowly along the seabed. The sunflower starfish travels at 0.06 kilometres (0.04 miles) per hour. It would need nearly an hour to cross an Olympic-sized swimming pool.

Feet help them eat

Starfish eat **molluscs** such as clams. To eat a clam, a starfish wraps its arms around the shell. Then it pries the shell open just a tiny bit with its tube feet. The starfish then pushes its stomach out of its mouth, through this small opening and into the clam shell. Then it **digests** the clam. This might take two days.

Most starfish have five arms. Sunflower starfish like this one, however, can have more than twenty.

Which snail really drags its foot?

Of all the snails in the world, the giant African land snail is one of the slowest. This snail glides along at about 0.006 kilometres (0.004 miles) per hour. It would take it 15 minutes to cross a wide pavement.

The giant African land snail leaves a trail of slime behind itself.

Travelling on foot

The Giant African land snail is a **mollusc** that is **native** to Africa. It has a cone-shaped shell up to 20 centimetres long that protects the snail's body. On the bottom of its body is a muscular structure called a foot. The muscles create a ripple effect along the foot, which pushes against the ground and moves the snail's body forward.

Not so fast!

One thing the giant African land snail can do quickly is **breed.** In a year, one snail can lay 1200 eggs. In 1966 a boy brought three giant African land snails into Florida, USA as pets. They were later turned loose in a garden. Seven years later, there were at least 18,000 of them in Florida!

The snails ate their way through a number of fruit and vegetable crops. It took the state of Florida nearly ten years to get rid of the snails. They have also spread to other parts of the world. In India, Southeast Asia and Hawaii they are an **invasive exotic species.** They **compete** with native snails for food. In most places where the snail has become established, attempts to get rid of it have failed.

This giant African land snail can lay about 200 to 500 eggs at a time.

Did you know?

The giant African land snail can survive cold temperatures by slowing down its bodily processes. It can save energy and wait until temperatures warm up again. This has helped it adapt to new and colder parts of the world.

Which insect might race you and win?

An American cockroach can scurry across a kitchen table in a second or less. As it runs, it zigzags quickly back and forth to avoid **predators.**

The cockroach has landed!

The American cockroach is actually **native** to Africa. Long ago cockroaches made their way on to ships in West Africa. They went wherever the ships took them. They arrived in the southern United States as early as 1625. Today they live in almost all parts of the world. Cockroaches are an **invasive exotic species.**

American cockroaches like to live in warm, moist dark areas, such as sewers, basements and boiler rooms. They need to be near water, so areas near toilets and baths are other places you might find them.

The American cockroach has strong wings and can fly long distances. But it is such a fast runner that it hardly ever uses its wings to get away from an enemy.

The secrets of success

One of the cockroach's **adaptations** for survival is that it can live just about anywhere. It will also eat whatever it can find. American cockroaches will eat human food, book bindings, wallpaper, hair, old shoes, dead insects and even other cockroaches. Cockroaches also **breed** very fast. A female lives a little longer than a year. During her lifetime she can produce about 150 young.

American cockroaches tend to live in places that are full of germs that cause diseases. The germs get on their bodies. When the cockroaches get into areas where food is stored or prepared, they can spread diseases to humans. People have tried everything from squashing to poisoning to starving cockroaches to get rid of them. Somehow, some cockroaches always seem to survive.

American cockroaches often gather in gigantic groups. More than 5000 have been found in a single sewer.

Did you know?

Cockroaches first appeared on Earth 320 million years ago. They have hardly changed since then.

Which flower might never bloom in your lifetime?

The *Puya raimondii* is a giant plant. There are stories that it takes 150 years to make a flower. But scientists think it blooms after 80 to 100 years. It is the slowest flower to bloom in the world.

It is thought that hummingbirds **pollinate** *the* Puya raimondii.

No shrinking violet

The *Puya raimondii* grows high in the meadows of the Andes Mountains in South America. It can grow up to 9 metres high. That is about as tall as a telephone pole. The giant flower can be 2.4 metres wide, but it is actually a cluster of about 8000 tiny flowers.

Did you know?

The *Puya raimondii* is a type of flower called a bromeliad. Pineapples are also bromeliads.

When can you see grass grow?

The giant timber bamboo can sometimes grow more than 1 metre in a day! It can reach a height of 17 metres in just a few years. That is almost as tall as a four-storey building.

The giant timber bamboo is a hollow, woody grass that is **native** to China. Spear-shaped leaves grow on branches near the top of the plant stems. It grows fast, but it can live for 120 years before blooming.

Bamboo in building

The giant timber bamboo has long been used as a building material in Asia. People use it to make fences, furniture and even houses.

In North America and Europe, people have started using bamboo instead of wood. Pine trees must grow at least ten to twenty years before they can be used. But bamboo can be harvested in three to five years. This can reduce the number of trees that are cut from the world's forests.

Giant timber bamboo is similar in strength to steel.

☑ The horned sungem is a hummingbird that lives in South America. It flaps its wings 90 times every second. That is faster than any other bird.

☑ The mimosa, or sensitive plant, can wilt in an instant. If a leaf is touched, it quickly folds up. If it is touched hard enough, there is a chain reaction and even leaves that were not directly touched will close. Sometimes even the stalk will crumple and wilt, right before your eyes!

☑ Certain types of African ants can clamp their mouthparts shut at a speed of 8.6 metres per second. That is the same as moving 30.5 kilometres (19 miles) per hour.

☑ Some woodpeckers can peck at a speed of 15 pecks per second, or about 900 times per minute.

☑ When flying, vultures flap their wings only once per second.

The Jackson's three-horned chameleon of Africa can flick its tongue out, grab an insect and pull its tongue and the insect back into its mouth in about half a second.

- An elephant's heart beats very slowly – only 25 times per minute. A mouse's heart beats 700 times per minute. The adult human heart beats on average 70 times per minute.

- One of the fastest flying insects is the desert locust. It can reach speeds of about 33.8 kilometres (21 miles) per hour. That is about twice as fast as most children can cycle.

- The basilisk lizards of Africa can run at a speed of about 11 kilometres (7 miles) per hour. This is fast enough for them to run across the surface of water without sinking.

The Venus flytrap is a type of plant that traps insects in its jaw-like leaves. When an insect brushes against the hairs on a flytrap leaf, the leaves snap completely shut within half a second. The plant then **digests** the insect.

Glossary

adaptation   special feature that helps a plant or animal survive

amphibian   animal that lives part of its life in water and part on land

bask   warm up in the sun

breed   when a male and female come together to make babies

camouflage   change the way something looks so it will not be easy to see

cold-blooded   has blood that is the same temperature as the surrounding air or water

compete   when two or more species go after the same food, water or shelter

defecate   excrete solid waste

digest   break down food so it can be absorbed by the body

dorsal fin   fin on the back of a fish and some marine mammals

echinoderm   sea animal without a backbone that often has a spiny shell. Sea stars and sea urchins are echinoderms.

endangered species   group of animals or plants that may die out soon

extinct   when no members of a species remain on Earth

gill   opening in a fish's or amphibian's body that lets it breathe underwater

habitat   place where an animal lives in the wild

invasive exotic species   plant or animal that has arrived in a new area and has spread and crowded out native species

larva   (plural is larvae) early stage in the life of a newt during which it lives in water and gradually grows legs and lungs

mammal   animal that is warm-blooded, has hair or fur, a backbone and drinks milk made by its mother

mate   partner with whom an animal makes babies

metamorphosis   change of an animal's body in size, shape and function

mollusc   soft-bodied animal that has no bones

native   plant or animal that has always lived in a particular area

nutrient   food substance that a plant or animal needs to survive

pollinate   carry a dusty substance (pollen) made by flowers from one part of a flower to another, or from one plant to another

predator   animal that hunts, kills and eats another type of animal

prey   animal that is hunted by other animals for food

rainforest   thick forest of tall trees where it rains almost every day

reptile   cold-blooded animal with a backbone and scaly skin that breathes through lungs and lays eggs

species   group of animals that have the same features and can have babies with each other

subspecies   group of related animals within a species

talon   sharp claw

urinate   pass liquid waste

vulnerable   species at risk of dying out. Vulnerable species are not at as great a risk of dying out as endangered species.

More books to read

Amazing Nature: Powerful Predators, Tim Knight (Heinemann Library, 2003)

Animals Under Threat: Peregrine Falcon, Mike Unwin (Heinemann Library, 2004)

Focus on the Living World, Jane Parker (Franklin Watts, 2003)

Totally Weird: Rainforests, Kate Graham (Raintree, 1999)

Wild Predators! Deadly Snakes, Andrew Solway (Heinemann Library, 2004)

Index